CW00862925

Naples Travel Tips
Exploring Naples with the
essential travel information
(Travel Guide)

Hudson Miles

All rights reserved. No part of
this publication may be
reproduced, distributed, or
transmitted in any form or by
any means, including
photocopying, recording, or
other electronic or mechanical
methods, without the prior
written permission of the
publisher, except in the case of
brief quotations embodied in
critical reviews and certain other
noncommercial uses permitted
by copyright law.

Copyright © Hudson Miles),
(2023).

Table Of Contents

Introduction

Welcome to the vibrant city of Naples, Italy's hidden gem nestled on the picturesque Bay of Naples. Bursting with history, art, culinary delights, and breathtaking coastal landscapes, Naples is a city that captivates the hearts of its visitors. From the ruins of Pompeii to the mesmerizing Amalfi Coast, this travel guide will be your companion in unraveling the secrets of this enchanting destination.

Step into the streets of Naples, and you'll be greeted by a vibrant tapestry of life. The city's rich heritage, dating back to ancient Greek and Roman times, is evident in its architecture, archaeology, and diverse cultural offerings. Stroll through the historic center, a UNESCO World Heritage Site, and get lost amidst narrow alleys adorned with charming balconies and colorful laundry lines. Marvel at the opulence of the Royal Palace of Naples or immerse yourself in the ancient world at the National Archaeological Museum, housing remarkable artifacts from Pompeii and Herculaneum.

But Naples is not just a city frozen in time. It pulsates with energy, and its people are known for their warmth and zest for life. Indulge in the vibrant Neapolitan street culture as you explore the bustling markets, such as the famous Via dei Tribunali, where the aroma of freshly baked pizza fills the air. Delight in authentic Neapolitan cuisine, savoring the iconic Margherita pizza, delectable seafood dishes, and the creamy delight of traditional sfogliatella pastries.

Beyond the city limits, Naples unveils its natural wonders. Embark on an adventure to the legendary Mount Vesuvius, the still-active volcano that overlooks the bay, offering awe-inspiring panoramic views. Explore the nearby ruins of Pompeii and Herculaneum, preserved in time by the volcanic ash, and discover the daily lives of ancient Romans.

And let's not forget the captivating Amalfi Coast, a short drive from Naples. With its dramatic cliffs, azure waters, and charming towns like Positano and Amalfi, this coastal paradise will leave you breathless. Immerse yourself in the laid-back atmosphere, unwind on sun-soaked beaches, and indulge in the region's world-renowned limoncello.

Whether you're a history enthusiast, a food lover, or a nature seeker, Naples offers an unparalleled blend of experiences that will leave a lasting impression. So, grab this travel guide and embark on a journey of discovery through the enchanting streets, rich heritage, and breathtaking landscapes of Naples, where history and modernity seamlessly intertwine.

Chapter 1

Introduction to Naples

Naples, or Napoli in Italian, is a vibrant city located in southern Italy. It is the capital of the Campania region and the third-largest city in Italy, known for its rich history, stunning architecture, and mouthwatering cuisine. With its strategic position overlooking the Bay of Naples and its proximity to iconic attractions like Pompeii and Mount Vesuvius, Naples is a popular destination for travelers seeking a unique and authentic Italian experience.

The city has a fascinating past that stretches back over 2,800 years, making it one of the oldest continuously inhabited cities in the world. It was founded by the Greeks in the 8th century BCE and later became a flourishing Roman city. Naples has witnessed the rise and fall of various civilizations, including the Byzantines,

Normans, Angevins, and Aragonese, which have all left their mark on the city's architecture and cultural heritage.

Naples is often referred to as an open-air museum due to its wealth of historic sites and landmarks. The historic center, a UNESCO World Heritage Site, is a maze of narrow streets, where grand palaces, ancient churches, and bustling piazzas coexist with local markets, shops, and vibrant street life. One of the highlights of Naples is the National Archaeological Museum, home to an extraordinary collection of ancient Greek and Roman artifacts, including the treasures of Pompeii and Herculaneum.

Beyond its historical significance, Naples is renowned for its culinary delights. It is the birthplace of the iconic Neapolitan pizza, which is considered one of the best pizzas in the world. The city is also famous for its mouth watering street food, such as fried pizza, arancini (rice balls), and the delectable pastries like sfogliatelle and babà. Neapolitans take their food seriously, and the city boasts numerous traditional pizzerias, trattorias, and family-run restaurants serving up authentic and flavorful dishes.

In addition to its urban charms, Naples offers breathtaking natural beauty. The imposing Mount Vesuvius dominates the skyline, inviting adventurous travelers to hike its slopes and witness panoramic views of the surrounding landscape. The nearby ruins of Pompeii and Herculaneum, both destroyed by the catastrophic eruption of Vesuvius in 79 CE, provide a unique glimpse into the daily life of ancient Romans.

Whether you're exploring the historic center, savoring mouthwatering cuisine, or embarking on day trips to nearby attractions, Naples is a city that captivates visitors with its distinct character and undeniable allure. Its combination of history, culture, and natural beauty makes it a must-visit destination for travelers seeking an authentic Italian experience.

Chapter 2

Top Attractions

When visiting Naples, you'll find a wealth of attractions that cater to various interests. Here are some of the top attractions to explore in the city:

Pompeii and Herculaneum:
Take a day trip to the ancient cities of Pompeii and Herculaneum, which were preserved by the eruption of Mount Vesuvius in 79 CE. Wander through remarkably well-preserved streets, admire ancient houses, and witness the daily life of the Romans.

Mount Vesuvius:
Embark on a thrilling hike up the slopes of Mount Vesuvius, an active volcano that overlooks the Bay of Naples. Enjoy panoramic views of the surrounding

countryside and peer into the volcano's crater.

Naples National Archaeological Museum:
Explore one of the world's most significant archaeological museums, housing an extensive collection of Greek and Roman artifacts. Marvel at the Farnese Hercules, the Toro Farnese, and the mosaics from Pompeii.

Castel dell'Ovo:
Visit the Castel dell'Ovo, an ancient seaside castle located on the islet of Megaride. Admire its medieval architecture, stroll along the promenade, and enjoy stunning views of the Bay of Naples and Mount Vesuvius.

Royal Palace of Naples:
Step inside the opulent Royal Palace of Naples, a magnificent palace that served as the residence of the Bourbon Kings. Explore

its lavish rooms, admire its stunning frescoes, and visit the Royal Armory.
San Gennaro Catacombs:

Descend into the underground world of the San Gennaro Catacombs, an ancient burial site that dates back to the 2nd century. Marvel at the intricate frescoes and learn about early Christian burial practices.

Certosa di San Martino:
Visit the Certosa di San Martino, a former monastery located atop the Vomero hill. Explore its stunning cloisters, admire the ornate Baroque architecture, and enjoy panoramic views of the city and the bay.

Naples Underground:
Discover the hidden side of Naples by exploring its underground tunnels and ancient aqueducts. Take a guided tour through the labyrinthine passages and learn about the city's fascinating subterranean history.

Galleria Umberto I:
Immerse yourself in the elegance of the Galleria Umberto I, a stunning 19th-century shopping gallery. Marvel at its glass dome, shop at luxury boutiques, and enjoy a coffee in one of the charming cafes.

Piazza del Plebiscito:
Visit the grand Piazza del Plebiscito, one of Naples' main squares. Admire the impressive Royal Palace, the majestic San Francesco di Paola church, and take a stroll along the palm-lined promenade.
These attractions offer a glimpse into the rich history, cultural heritage, and natural wonders of Naples. Each one contributes to the unique charm and allure of the city.

Chapter 3

Neighborhoods and Districts

Naples is a city of diverse neighborhoods and districts, each with its own distinct character and charm. Exploring these areas will give you a deeper understanding of the city's vibrant culture and history. Here are some notable neighborhoods and districts in Naples:

Historic Center (Centro Storico):
The heart of Naples, Centro Storico is a UNESCO World Heritage Site and a bustling hub of activity. Wander through narrow, winding streets lined with colorful buildings, visit historic churches, and explore vibrant markets like the bustling Via San Gregorio Armeno, famous for its nativity scene artisans.

Spaccanapoli:

Spaccanapoli is a long and narrow street that cuts through the historic center of Naples, dividing it into two parts. Stroll along this atmospheric street and discover shops selling traditional crafts, local eateries serving authentic Neapolitan cuisine, and historic sites like the Church of Santa Chiara and San Domenico Maggiore.

Chiaia:
Chiaia is an elegant and upscale neighborhood located along the seafront. It is known for its beautiful palaces, upscale shopping streets like Via Chiaia, and stylish boutiques. Enjoy a leisurely stroll along the Lungomare promenade, relax in the Villa Comunale park, and indulge in the neighborhood's refined dining scene.

Posillipo:
Situated on a picturesque hill overlooking the Bay of Naples, Posillipo offers breathtaking views and a tranquil atmosphere. Explore its winding streets,

admire the elegant villas, and visit the Parco Virgiliano, a scenic park with panoramic views of the bay and the islands of Capri, Ischia, and Procida.

Vomero:

Vomero is a hilltop district that offers stunning panoramic views of Naples. It is known for its upscale residential areas, trendy cafes, and lively shopping streets like Via Scarlatti and Via Luca Giordano. Visit the Castel Sant'Elmo fortress and the nearby Certosa di San Martino for a glimpse into the district's history.

Spanish Quarter (Quartieri Spagnoli):

The Spanish Quarter is a vibrant and lively neighborhood known for its narrow, bustling streets and colorful buildings. Immerse yourself in local life as you explore the neighborhood's vibrant markets, small shops, and lively piazzas. Experience the authentic atmosphere and sample traditional street food.

Materdei:

Materdei is a historic neighborhood that offers a glimpse into the past of Naples. Explore its narrow alleys, admire the beautiful baroque church of Santa Maria di Materdei, and visit the Basilica of Santa Maria della Sanità, famous for its stunning frescoes.

Each neighborhood in Naples has its own unique atmosphere, architecture, and attractions. Exploring these districts will provide you with a diverse and enriching experience of the city's vibrant culture and history.

Chapter 4

Food and Drink

When it comes to food and drink, Naples is a culinary paradise. The city is renowned for its mouthwatering cuisine, which includes iconic dishes, delightful street food, and a strong coffee culture. Here are some highlights of the food and drink scene in Naples:

Neapolitan Pizza:
Naples is the birthplace of pizza, and it's a must-try when visiting the city. Sample authentic Neapolitan pizza, characterized by its thin, soft crust and high-quality ingredients. Pizzerias like Sorbillo, Da Michele, and Di Matteo are famous for serving some of the best pizzas in Naples.

Street Food:
Naples boasts a vibrant street food culture. Savor local specialties like fried pizza (pizza

fritta), a deep-fried dough filled with delicious toppings, and arancini, fried rice balls usually stuffed with ragù (meat sauce) or mozzarella. Other popular street food items include cuoppo (fried seafood), panino napoletano (Neapolitan sandwich), and zeppole (sweet fried dough balls).

Seafood:
Being a coastal city, Naples offers an abundance of fresh seafood dishes. Sample delights like spaghetti alle vongole (spaghetti with clams), frittura di paranza (mixed fried seafood), and pesce al forno (oven-baked fish). The waterfront neighborhoods, such as Santa Lucia and Mergellina, are excellent places to enjoy seafood specialties.

Neapolitan Pastries:
Naples is famous for its delectable pastries. Indulge in treats like sfogliatella, a flaky pastry filled with sweet ricotta cream or semolina, and babà, a rum-soaked sponge

cake. Other favorites include pastiera, a traditional Easter cake with ricotta and candied fruit, and struffoli, honey-coated dough balls.

Coffee Culture:
Naples has a strong coffee culture, and visiting a traditional Neapolitan coffee house, known as a caffè, is a must. Order a classic espresso or try the local specialty, caffè sospeso, which involves paying for an extra coffee to be given to a stranger in need. Enjoy the rich flavors and aroma while savoring the relaxed atmosphere of a historic caffè.

Gelato:
Cool off with a scoop or two of authentic Neapolitan gelato. Naples has numerous gelaterias offering a wide variety of flavors made with fresh, high-quality ingredients. Look out for traditional flavors like stracciatella (chocolate chip), pistachio, and fiordilatte (sweet milk).

Traditional Neapolitan Dishes:
Naples is home to a range of traditional dishes that showcase the region's culinary heritage. Try pasta dishes like spaghetti alle acciughe (spaghetti with anchovies) and pasta e patate (pasta with potatoes). Sample local cheeses like mozzarella di bufala, and savor dishes like parmigiana di melanzane (eggplant parmesan) and polpette (meatballs) in tomato sauce.

Local Wines and Liqueurs:
Naples and the Campania region produce excellent wines. Try the famous Lacryma Christi, a white or red wine made from grapes grown on the slopes of Mount Vesuvius. Limoncello, a lemon liqueur, is also popular in Naples and makes for a refreshing after-dinner drink.
Food and drink are an integral part of the Neapolitan culture, and indulging in the city's culinary offerings is a delightful experience that shouldn't be missed during your visit.

Chapter 5

Day Trips and Excursions

While exploring Naples, you'll find plenty of opportunities for day trips and excursions to nearby destinations. Here are some popular options for day trips from Naples:

Amalfi Coast:
Embark on a scenic drive along the stunning Amalfi Coast, a UNESCO World Heritage Site. Visit picturesque towns like Positano, Amalfi, and Ravello, known for their colorful houses, beautiful beaches, and charming coastal atmosphere.

Capri:
Take a ferry from Naples to the glamorous island of Capri. Explore the glamorous town of Capri, visit the stunning Blue Grotto (Grotta Azzurra), take a chairlift up to Monte Solaro for panoramic views, and relax in the famous Piazzetta.

Ischia:
Escape to the island of Ischia, known for its thermal spas and natural beauty. Relax in the island's thermal baths, visit the Aragonese Castle, explore the lush gardens of La Mortella, and enjoy the sandy beaches.

Procida:
Visit the charming island of Procida, located in the Bay of Naples. Wander through the pastel-colored houses and narrow streets of the historic center, visit the Terra Murata fortress, and relax on the island's picturesque beaches.

Caserta Royal Palace:
Take a trip to the magnificent Caserta Royal Palace (Reggia di Caserta), a grand palace often referred to as the "Versailles of Italy." Explore the opulent interiors, admire the beautiful gardens, and learn about the palace's rich history.
Vesuvius National Park:

Venture to Vesuvius National Park and hike to the summit of Mount Vesuvius, an active volcano. Enjoy panoramic views of the surrounding landscape and visit the volcanic crater to witness the power of nature up close.

Sorrento:
Explore the charming town of Sorrento, located on the Sorrentine Peninsula. Wander through the narrow streets lined with shops selling local crafts and limoncello, visit the scenic Piazza Tasso, and enjoy stunning views of the Bay of Naples.

These day trips from Naples offer a chance to explore the stunning coastline, visit islands with natural beauty, immerse yourself in history, and experience the charm of nearby towns. Whether you're seeking relaxation, adventure, or cultural exploration, these excursions provide a diverse range of experiences just a short distance from Naples.

Chapter 6

Cultural Experiences

Naples is a city rich in culture and offers a variety of experiences that allow visitors to immerse themselves in its vibrant heritage. Here are some cultural experiences to enjoy in Naples:

Opera at Teatro di San Carlo:
Experience the magic of opera by attending a performance at Teatro di San Carlo, one of the oldest and most prestigious opera houses in the world. Enjoy the stunning architecture and the melodious voices of talented opera singers.

Museums and Art Galleries:
Explore Naples' art and history by visiting its museums and art galleries. Apart from the National Archaeological Museum, which houses an impressive collection of ancient artifacts, you can also visit the Capodimonte

Museum, featuring works by Italian masters, and the Naples Contemporary Art Museum (MADRE), showcasing modern and contemporary art.

Neapolitan Music and Dance:
Immerse yourself in Neapolitan music and dance, which is deeply rooted in the city's cultural heritage. Attend a traditional folk music performance, listen to street musicians playing the mandolin and accordion, or watch a lively tarantella dance performance.

Historical Churches:
Naples is home to numerous stunning churches that showcase exquisite art and architecture. Visit the Duomo di San Gennaro, the city's main cathedral, and witness the miracle of the liquefaction of the saint's blood. Other notable churches include the Church of Santa Chiara, with its beautiful majolica-tiled cloister, and the

Gesù Nuovo Church, known for its impressive marble facade.
Street Life and Local Markets:

Naples has a vibrant street life that reflects the city's unique character. Wander through lively markets like the colorful street of Via San Gregorio Armeno, famous for its nativity scene artisans, and the Mercato di Porta Nolana, where locals sell fresh produce and seafood. Observe daily life, interact with the locals, and soak up the lively atmosphere.

Traditional Festivals:
Experience the city's festive spirit by participating in traditional festivals. The Feast of San Gennaro, celebrated on September 19th, is a major religious festival dedicated to Naples' patron saint. Witness the processions, street performances, and fireworks that take place during this vibrant event.

Neapolitan Cuisine:

Naples' culinary heritage is an integral part of its culture. Take a cooking class to learn how to make authentic Neapolitan dishes like pizza, pasta, and pastries. Visit local markets and food shops to discover the ingredients that make Neapolitan cuisine so special.

Local Neighborhoods:

Explore the different neighborhoods of Naples, each with its own distinct character and cultural traditions. Wander through the narrow streets of the Spanish Quarter (Quartieri Spagnoli), mingle with the locals in the lively Forcella neighborhood, and discover the vibrant art scene in the Sanità neighborhood.

These cultural experiences will give you a deeper appreciation for the rich heritage and vibrant spirit of Naples. Embrace the city's traditions, interact with the locals, and indulge in its cultural offerings to make your visit a truly immersive and memorable one.

Chapter 7

Practical Information

When traveling to Naples, it's helpful to have some practical information to ensure a smooth and enjoyable trip. Here are some key practical tips for your visit to Naples:

Best Time to Visit:
The best time to visit Naples is during the spring (April to June) and fall (September to October) when the weather is mild, and there are fewer crowds. Summers can be hot and crowded, while winters tend to be mild but with occasional rain.

Getting Around:
Naples has an extensive public transportation system that includes buses, trams, and a metro system. The metro is a convenient way to travel within the city and to reach neighboring areas. Taxis and rideshare services are also available.

Safety:

Like any major city, it's important to take precautions for your safety. Be mindful of your belongings and avoid displaying valuable items openly. It's advisable to be cautious in crowded areas and use well-lit streets, especially at night.

Currency and Payment:

The currency used in Naples is the Euro (EUR). Credit cards are widely accepted in hotels, restaurants, and shops, but it's always good to have some cash on hand for small purchases and places that may not accept cards.

Language:

The official language of Naples is Italian. While English is spoken in many tourist areas, it's helpful to learn a few basic Italian phrases or carry a translation app to communicate with locals.

Tipping:

Tipping is not as common in Italy as it is in some other countries. However, it's customary to leave a small tip if you're pleased with the service. A typical tip is around 5-10% of the total bill.

Dress Code:
Naples is a stylish city, and locals generally dress well. However, there is no strict dress code, and casual attire is acceptable in most places. When visiting churches or religious sites, it's respectful to dress modestly and cover your shoulders and knees.

Electrical Outlets:
The standard voltage in Naples is 230V, and the power plugs and sockets are of type F (two round pins). If your appliances use a different type of plug, you may need a travel adapter.

Emergency Numbers:
In case of an emergency, dial 112 to reach the general emergency services in Italy,

including police, fire, and medical assistance.

Remember to check the latest information and guidelines before your trip to Naples, as conditions and regulations may change. By being well-prepared and informed, you can make the most of your visit to this captivating city.

Chapter 8

practical tips

Certainly! Here are some practical tips to enhance your experience while visiting Naples:

Plan Sufficient Time: Naples offers a wide range of attractions and experiences, so plan your itinerary accordingly to make the most of your visit. Allocate ample time for sightseeing, exploring neighborhoods, and enjoying the local cuisine.

Dress Comfortably: Naples involves a lot of walking, so wear comfortable shoes and lightweight clothing. The city's streets can be uneven, so opt for sturdy footwear to navigate the cobblestone streets with ease.

Stay Hydrated: Naples can get hot, especially during the summer months. Carry a refillable water bottle and drink plenty of fluids to stay hydrated while exploring the city.

Be Mindful of Pickpockets: As in any tourist destination, be cautious of pickpockets. Keep an eye on your belongings, especially in crowded areas and public transportation. Use a money belt or secure bag to safeguard your valuables.

Learn Basic Italian Phrases: While many locals in tourist areas speak English, learning a few basic Italian phrases can go a long way in interacting with locals and showing respect for the local culture. Simple greetings like "buongiorno" (good morning) and "grazie" (thank you) are always appreciated.

Sample Local Cuisine: Naples is known for its incredible food, so take advantage of the opportunity to try traditional Neapolitan dishes. Seek out local pizzerias, street food vendors, and authentic trattorias for an authentic culinary experience.

Use Public Transportation: Naples has a well-connected public transportation system, including buses, trams, and metro lines. Consider using public transport to navigate the city efficiently. Purchase a rechargeable transport card (e.g., the Naples Unico Campania card) for convenience and cost savings.

Validate Tickets: If you choose to use public transportation, remember to validate your ticket in the designated machines upon boarding buses or entering metro stations. Failure to validate your ticket may result in a fine if inspected.

Take Note of Siesta Time: Naples, like many cities in Italy, observes a siesta period in the afternoon. During this time, some shops and businesses may close for a few hours. Plan your activities accordingly and take advantage of this quieter period to relax or enjoy a leisurely meal.

Embrace the Local Pace: Naples has a unique energy and a more relaxed pace of life. Embrace the laid-back atmosphere, and allow yourself to immerse in the city's vibrant culture and the warmth of its people.

By keeping these practical tips in mind, you can have a more enjoyable and hassle-free experience during your visit to Naples.